True Tales™
of
Burning Earth

Henry Billings
Melissa Stone Billings

STECK-VAUGHN
ELEMENTARY · SECONDARY · ADULT · LIBRARY
A Harcourt Company

www.steck-vaughn.com

Acknowledgments

Editorial Director: Stephanie Muller
Senior Editor: Kristy Schulz
Associate Director of Design: Cynthia Ellis
Design Manager: Alexandra Corona
Production Coordinator: Rebecca Gonzales
Media Researcher: Claudette Landry
Page Production Artist: Dina Bahan
Cover Production Artist: Dina Bahan

Cartography: Pp. 4–5, 7, 15, 23, 31, 39, 47, 55, 63, 71, 79, 87, 95, MapQuest.com, Inc.
Illustration Credits: Pp. 13, 29, 37, 45, 53, 61, 69, 77, 85, 93, 101, Eulala Conner
Photo Credits: Cover (background) ©PhotoDisc; front cover (inset) ©David Frazier/SIPA Press; back cover (spot) ©John T. Barr/Liaison Agency, Inc.; p.3 ©PhotoDisc; p.6 ©Jonathen Blair/CORBIS; pp.8, 9 (both), 10 from Memorials of the Minnesota Forest Fires by William Wilkinson; p.14 ©Tony Roberts/CORBIS; p.16 Courtesy U.S. Golf Association; p.17 ©Davis Factor/CORBIS; p.18(t) ©Bettmann/CORBIS; p.18(b) ©J.D. Cuban/Allsport; pp.22-25 ©David DeKok; p.26 ©Leif Skoogfors/CORBIS; p.30 ©The Seattle Times; p.32 ©Kenneth Garrett/National Geographic Image Collection; p.33 ©PhotoDisc; p.34 ©Kenneth Garrett/National Geographic Image Collection; pp.38, 40(b) Courtesy Nicholas Schneider; p.40(t) Courtesy Linda Casagrande; p.41(t) ©University of Texas Southwestern Medical Center at Dallas; p.41(b) (c)PhotoDisc; p.42 Courtesy Nicholas Schneider; p.46 ©Steven L. Raymer/National Geographic Image Collection; p.48(b) ©Steven L. Raymer/National Geographic Image Collection; p.48(t) ©D. Goldberg/Sygma; p.49 ©Latin Focus; p.50 ©J. Langevin/Sygma; p.54 ©Galen Rowell/CORBIS; p.56 ©Phil Degginger/Earth Scenes; p.57 ©PhotoDisc; p.58 Los Angeles Times Photo; p.62 ©Les Stone/Sygma; p.64 ©Roger Ressmeyer/CORBIS; p.65 ©Melvyn Calderon/Liaison Agency, Inc.; p.66(t) ©Kees/Sygma; p.66(b) ©Sigfred Balatan/Black Star; p.70 ©Ventura County Newspapers/Liaison Agency, Inc.; p.72 ©Ken Levine/I.M.E./SIPA Press; p.73 ©Mooney/SIPA Press; p.74 ©John T. Barr/Liaison Agency, Inc.; p.78 ©Eric Lars Bakks/Black Star; p.80 Courtesy the Holtby Family; p.81 ©Aaron Strong/Liaison Agency, Inc.; p.82 ©Eric Lars Bakks/Black Star; p.86 ©Ingrid Van Den Berg/Earth Scenes; p.88 (both) Reuters/Etienne Rothbart/Archive Photos; p.89 ©Anthony Bannister; Gallo Images/CORBIS; p.90 ©David Thompson/Animals Animals; p.94 ©Savino/SIPA Press; p.96 ©De Keerle/FSP/Liaison Agency, Inc.; p.97 ©Patrick Robert/Sygma; p.98 ©Savino/SIPA Press; p.108(t) Courtesy NASA; p.108(m) ©PhotoDisc; p.108(b) ©Marc Deville/Liaison Agency, Inc.; p.109(t) Popperfoto; p.109(m) ©SIPA Press; p.109(b) ©Tom Ives/The Stock Market.

ISBN 0-7398-2390-6

1 2 3 4 5 6 7 8 9 10 DBH 04 03 02 01 00

Contents

ARCTIC OCEAN

NORTH AMERICA

Hinckley, Minnesota, 1894
Oak Brook, Illinois, 1975
Mt. Whitney, California, 1990
Centralia, Pennsylvania, 1981
Southern California, 1993
Glenwood Springs, Colorado, 1994

PACIFIC OCEAN

Arlington, Texas, 1984

ATLANTIC

OCEAN

El Chichón, Mexico, 1982
Montserrat, Caribbean Sea, 1997

Armero, Colombia, 1985

Equator

SOUTH AMERICA

ATLAN

OCEA

Map Key

- forest fire
- lightning
- underground coal fire
- volcano
- grass fire

arth

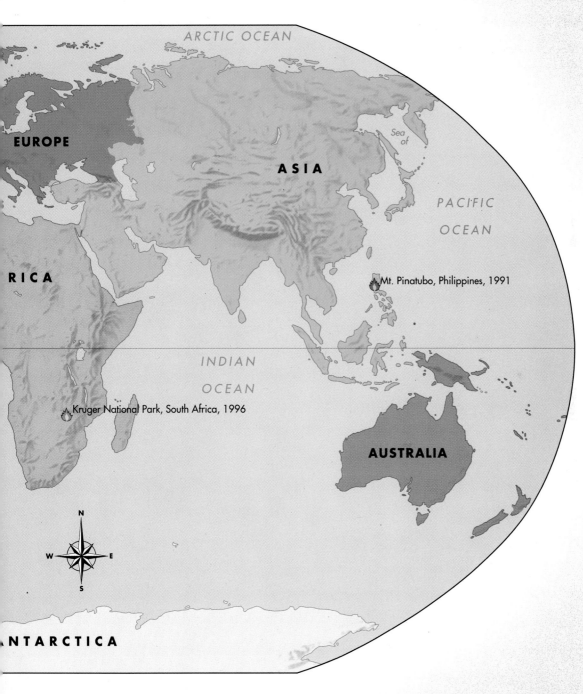

ARCTIC OCEAN

EUROPE

ASIA

Sea of

PACIFIC
OCEAN

RICA

Mt. Pinatubo, Philippines, 1991

INDIAN
OCEAN

Kruger National Park, South Africa, 1996

AUSTRALIA

N
W E
S

NTARCTICA

Race Through the Flames

ollie McNeill looked out the window of her home on September 2, 1894. She could barely believe what she saw. A huge forest fire was sweeping toward the town of Hinckley, Minnesota. Within minutes it would reach her house. McNeill rushed outside. She began running down the railroad tracks that led out of town. More than 200 other people were doing the same thing. But the fire was closing in on them. McNeill wasn't sure if any of them would make it out alive.

A Race for Life

Soon McNeill saw flames ahead of her. They formed a huge, roaring wall of fire. Heat **radiated** out from the flames. These waves of heat hit McNeill's face. Still, she kept running.

"How I ever got through I do not know," she later said. "People were falling on every side of me. Twice my dress caught fire."

As McNeill ran, the fire continued to spread. The dry trees and bushes around Hinckley made the perfect **fuel**. So once the fire was **ignited**, it kept getting bigger and bigger.

About a mile north of Hinckley, McNeill saw something in the distance. She struggled to see through the smoke. A train called the *Limited* was on its way into the town. McNeill ran as fast as she could toward it. The train seemed like her only chance of escaping the fire.

Jim Root was the **engineer** of the *Limited*. He saw people racing toward him. He also saw the fire moving closer and closer. As McNeill and the others reached him, Root stopped the train. He helped them climb on board. Then he started the *Limited* moving again.

Soon, though, the train could go no farther. Roaring flames covered the tracks. Root began backing up the *Limited* as fast as possible. He knew that if he stopped the train, everyone on board would die in the **blaze**.

As the *Limited* moved backward, fire burned all around it. Soon parts of the train were on fire, too. Heat and smoke filled the air. Root's clothes caught on fire. Flames burned his face and arms. Yet he never let go of the **controls**. He continued to drive the train. Root wanted to save the people on the train even if it killed him.

Saving Lives

People on board were going crazy with fear. They screamed and cried. Some tried to beat the flames away with pieces of clothing. Others simply held their faces in their hands. Some people tried to jump out

The *Limited* was many people's only chance of escaping the fire.

Jim Root

John Blair

the doors. But leaving the train meant certain death. So a few brave people blocked the doors.

John Blair, a **porter**, saved many people on board the train. He told them to lie down on the floor. Since heat rises, that was the coolest place to be. Also, the heat was breaking the train's windows. People on the floor were less likely to be hit by flying glass.

Blair knew the train was powered by **steam**. The water **vapor** from the steam is what drove the train's engines. Blair knew there was a water tank on board. He rushed to get water from the tank. Then he raced through the train pouring water on people's heads and clothing.

Skunk Lake

After backing up for six miles, the *Limited* finally reached Skunk Lake. The lake wasn't much more than a muddy puddle. But it was wet and cool. It seemed like the best place to stop. Besides, Root couldn't hold the controls any longer. He was almost dead. He barely had enough strength to turn off the steam. Then he sank to the engine floor. He was badly burned. He was also bleeding from cuts caused by flying glass.

Two men pulled Root from the train. They carried him through the smoke and flames until they reached the lake. Then they set him down in the water and covered him with mud. Other people also stumbled off the train toward the lake. Many had been very badly burned. They were gasping for air in the heavy smoke. When they reached the dirty water, they threw their burned bodies in it.

When Mollie McNeill got to Skunk Lake, she sank down into the water. "I put my face in the mud to cool it," she said. "Someone **plastered** mud all over my hair."

For hours, McNeill, Root, Blair, and the others stayed in the water. All night long, the fire burned around them. They kept slapping mud on their skin to stay cool. As the mud dried, they put on more and more.

By morning, the fire finally died out. By then, 418 people lay dead. Most of the people who had been on the *Limited*, however, were still alive. Even Jim Root made it. It took Root months to get over his cuts and burns. But he was pleased to know that he had helped save the lives of so many people.

Skunk Lake did not have much water, but it kept people safe from the fire.

Read and Remember — Check the Events

Place a check in front of the three sentences that tell what happened in the story.

_____ **1.** Mollie McNeill ran away from Skunk Lake.

_____ **2.** The engineer asked someone to help drive the train.

_____ **3.** Jim Root backed up the train for six miles.

_____ **4.** Mollie McNeill ran away from her house in Hinckley, Minnesota.

_____ **5.** Jim Root's clothes caught on fire.

_____ **6.** No one on the *Limited* lived through the fire.

Write About It

Imagine you are a newspaper reporter in 1894. You are about to interview engineer Jim Root. Write three questions you would like to ask him.

1. _____

_____

_____

2. _____

_____

_____

3. _____

_____

_____

Focus on Vocabulary — Finish the Paragraphs

Use the words in dark print to complete the paragraphs.
Reread the paragraphs to be sure they make sense.

fuel	**porter**	**vapor**	**plastered**	**controls**
ignited	**radiated**	**engineer**	**blaze**	**steam**

On September 2, 1894, a **(1)**_____ began in Minnesota. Once the fire had been **(2)**_____, it spread quickly. There was plenty of **(3)**_____ to keep the fire burning. This huge fire **(4)**_____ a lot of heat. Soon it reached the town of Hinckley, Minnesota.

A train called the *Limited* was headed for Hinckley. Jim Root was the train's **(5)**_____. The train was powered by **(6)**_____. Water **(7)**_____ drove the engines. But Root was the one who handled the **(8)**_____.

To save the people on board, Root backed the train up. John Blair was a **(9)**_____ on the train. He poured water on people to cool them down. Later, people on board the train ran to a lake and **(10)**_____ themselves with mud.

Forest Fires

Forest fires can burn quickly. Twigs and dried leaves act as a **fuse** to start trees burning. The burning trees act as a chimney. They help push hot, smoky air upward. Fresh air is pulled into the fire, letting it continue to burn. Study the diagram. Write the answer to each question.

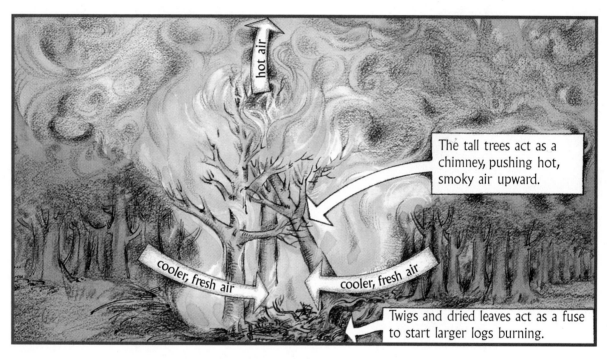

The tall trees act as a chimney, pushing hot, smoky air upward.

Twigs and dried leaves act as a fuse to start larger logs burning.

1. What acts as a fuse to start a fire? _____

2. What kind of air is pulled into a fire to keep it burning?

   _____

3. Does hot air move upward or downward? _____

   _____

4. How do the tall trees act as a chimney? _____

   _____

5. Does smoke stay at the bottom of the fire? _____

6. How do you think wind might affect a fire? _____

   _____

Trouble on the Golf Course

Lee Trevino really didn't mind the rain. Trevino was a **professional** golfer. He was often caught out on the golf course when it started to rain. He usually just opened his umbrella and kept playing. Trevino didn't mind thunder and **lightning**, either. "The lightning doesn't bother me," he said in June of 1975. But one week after saying that, Lee Trevino was in Oak Brook, Illinois. There he learned just how dangerous lightning could be.

A Storm on the Way

On June 27th, Trevino was at the Butler National Golf Club. He was playing in the Western Open Golf **Tournament**. Many other top golfers were also there.

Thousands of fans had come to cheer on the players. Fans especially loved Lee Trevino. He was more than just a great golfer. He also liked to joke around. That made him lots of fun to watch.

At 4 P.M. Trevino was on the 13th hole. He saw the sky turning dark. It looked like a **thunderstorm** was moving in. Other golfers saw the same thing. "There was a **rumbling** in the sky," said golfer Tony Jacklin. "But I thought it seemed a long way off." Still, the people running the tournament decided to stop the golfers from playing until the storm passed.

Like many others, Trevino waited out on the course for the storm to blow by. He thought he would be playing again in a few minutes. In the meantime, he was hungry. So he turned to Ned Garmoe. Garmoe was the **caddie** who carried Trevino's golf bag.

Trevino loved to play golf in all kinds of weather.

Trevino asked Garmoe if he would get him a hot dog and soda from a nearby snack bar.

A Strong Heart

As Garmoe walked off, Trevino sat down on the grass. He held an umbrella over his head and leaned back against his golf bag. He was still sitting there as Garmoe headed back toward him.

Suddenly lightning flashed across the sky. It hit the ground right near Trevino. The lightning traveled along the wet ground. From there, it entered into Trevino's body.

Lightning is a very powerful form of **electricity**. It is strong enough to stop a person's heart. It can also harm a person's brain. It can burn the human body. Lightning travels very fast. It moves 90,000 miles per second. If lightning finds a way out of the body quickly, it may not do too much **damage**.

In Lee Trevino's case, the lightning did leave quickly. It traveled out his back to the golf bag he was leaning against. Still, it was in his body long enough to cause problems. "The electricity stopped my heart," he later said. "The doctor said if I hadn't had such a strong heart, I would be dead."

Close to Dying

When Trevino first fell to the ground, no one knew what had happened. "I thought he was kidding around," said Garmoe.

Golf course worker Anna Grassel thought the same thing. "He rolled over a couple of times," said Grassel. "I thought he was kidding at first. Then he yelled, 'I've been hit!'"

Fans began running out onto the grass to help Trevino. By the time they reached him, his heart had started beating again. "He was **conscious**, but very scared," said Grassel. "He thought he was going to die. He said his whole life was passing before him." Trevino couldn't stop shaking. "I was in pain," Trevino later said. He felt like his whole body was exploding.

Trevino was lucky to be alive after the lightning struck.

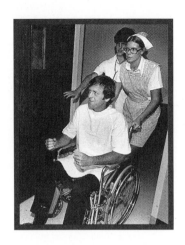

Bobby Nichols

Trevino was rushed to the hospital. Meanwhile, other golfers headed to the clubhouse. Lightning had hurt some of them, too. It knocked a golf club right out of Jim Ahern's hands. Said Ahern, "I felt a **shock** throughout my body. I just ran for the clubhouse, thankful to be alive."

Lightning knocked Bobby Nichols to the ground. "I've never been so scared in my life," Nichols said. When Nichols got up, he felt strange. His head hurt and he had a bad taste in his mouth. His breath smelled like burned wires. When doctors looked at him, they found lightning burns on his head.

Luckily, no one was killed by the lightning. Lee Trevino went on to play many more years as a top golfer. Still, he never forgot what had happened. From time to time he even joked about it. But he knew he had come close to dying out there on that golf course.

Trevino continued to play golf, but he never forgot about what happened.

Read and Remember — Choose the Answer

Draw a circle around the correct answer.

1. What did Trevino want from the snack bar?
   change for a dollar   a hot dog and soda   ice cream

2. Why did Trevino stop playing golf on the 13th hole?
   It started to rain.   He was tired.   He broke a club.

3. What did the lightning do to Trevino's heart?
   stopped it   burned it   made it grow

4. What did golf course worker Anna Grassel think Trevino was doing?
   kidding around   taking a nap   looking at the grass

5. What did Bobby Nichols's breath smell like?
   cotton candy   wet grass   burned wires

6. Where did the other golfers go during the lightning storm?
   to a nearby pond   to the clubhouse   to the snack bar

Think About It — Find the Main Ideas

Underline the two most important ideas from the story.

1. The fans loved Lee Trevino.

2. Trevino was struck by lightning.

3. Ned Garmoe worked for Lee Trevino.

4. Lightning traveled through Trevino's golf bag.

5. Trevino was lucky to survive.

6. Jim Ahern played golf with Lee Trevino.

Focus on Vocabulary — Find the Meaning

Read each sentence. Circle the best meaning for the word in dark print.

1. Trevino was a **professional** golfer.

   expert   person who has fun   easy to talk to

2. Lee Trevino was not scared of **lightning**.

   loud sound   flash of light in the sky   heavy rain

3. He was playing in a **tournament**.

   fancy place   lighted building   sports contest

4. A **thunderstorm** was moving in.

   wind with dirt   storm with thunder   white cloud

5. There was a **rumbling** in the sky.

   deep rolling sound   group of rain clouds   strange light

6. Garmoe was Trevino's **caddie**.

   old friend   golf partner   person who carries golf bags

7. **Electricity** can stop a person's heart.

   kind of energy   change of temperature   sickness

8. It did not do too much **damage**.

   moving around   harm   running

9. He was **conscious** but very scared.

   quiet   awake   trying very hard

10. He felt a **shock** throughout his body.

    charge of electric energy   chill   wave

Types of Lightning

People are amazed to see streaks of **lightning** during a thunderstorm. The giant electric sparks can come in different types. The chart below tells about five forms of lightning. Study the information. Circle the answer to each question.

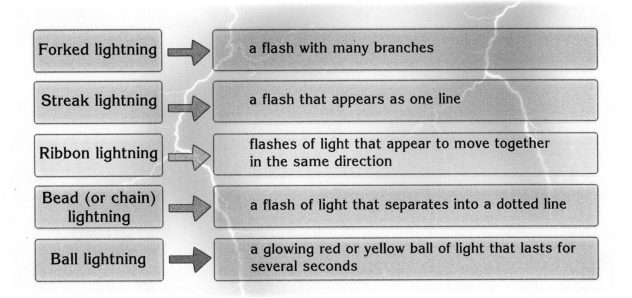

Forked lightning	a flash with many branches
Streak lightning	a flash that appears as one line
Ribbon lightning	flashes of light that appear to move together in the same direction
Bead (or chain) lightning	a flash of light that separates into a dotted line
Ball lightning	a glowing red or yellow ball of light that lasts for several seconds

1. What type of lightning seems to have many branches?

ribbon   bead   forked

2. What does streak lightning look like?

many lines   a single line   bright clouds

3. What type of lightning looks like flashes that move alongside one another?

forked   ribbon   group

4. What is another name for bead lightning?

chain lightning   ball lightning   bubble lightning

5. What type of lightning does **not** look like lines in the sky?

box lightning   bead lightning   ball lightning

The Fire That Keeps Burning

Twelve-year-old Todd Domboski wasn't doing anything dangerous. He was just walking through a backyard near his home in Centralia, Pennsylvania. His cousin, Eric Wolfgang, was with him. It was Valentine's Day, 1981, and the boys were visiting their grandmother. They did not know that they were walking across ground that held a terrible danger. Suddenly the ground underneath Todd opened up. He felt himself falling into a deep hole.

A Close Call

As Todd fell, he managed to grab hold of a tree root. Steam was coming up out of the hole. It was rising all around him. Luckily, Eric saw what was happening. He rushed over to the hole. Lying on his stomach, Eric grabbed Todd's hand and pulled him out of the hole to safety.

Later Todd learned just how close he had come to dying. As he hung from the tree root, he had faced three dangers. First, he could have fallen to the bottom of the hole. **Officials** later said it went 280 feet down into the ground. Second, Todd could have burned to death. The air deep in the hole was 450° **Fahrenheit**. Such heat would quickly kill a person. Third, Todd could have died from the steam rising out of the hole. The steam was really **poisonous** gas. It would have killed Todd within two or three minutes.

Todd was terribly frightened by what had happened. He and his family soon moved out of Centralia. He would never look at his old town the same way again. "When I used to think of Centralia, I thought of a nice quiet town," he said in 1982. "When I think about it now, I just get this feeling of **evil**."

What kind of strange place was it that nearly killed Todd Domboski? The hot, steaming hole was caused by a **coal** fire deep under the ground. Everyone in Centralia knew about the fire. It had been burning for close to 19 years. But this was the first time the fire had almost killed someone.

A Big Problem

The fire was first discovered on May 29, 1962. A man saw smoke rising from an old coal mining pit. People in town had been using the open pit as a garbage dump. Somehow a fire broke out in the dump. No one knows how it started. In any case, it began as an ordinary fire. But then it spread to a **seam** of coal. The seam ran into the ground. As the fire spread along this seam, it went deeper and deeper underground.

Todd Domboski and his family left Centralia soon after he fell into the hole.

24

Few people live in Centralia because the fire is still burning there.

When the fire moved underground, it became a real problem. Centralia was once a coal-mining town. There were still hundreds of mining **tunnels** underneath the town. Once the fire got into these tunnels, it was almost impossible to stop. There was plenty of coal to feed the fire. Also, there was lots of **oxygen** to keep it burning.

The fire burned holes up through the surface of the earth. That weakened the ground. Sometimes the ground just caved in. It was this kind of **sinkhole** that almost killed Todd Domboski. Sinkholes also cracked the walls of houses. Sometimes they caused whole houses to cave in.

The fire caused Route 61 to split open once. Smoke and heat rose out of the crack. It was so bad the road had to be closed. The fire also caused many trees to dry up and die. The heat from the ground killed the roots. In addition, poisonous gas leaked up into homes. Many people in Centralia said the gas was making them sick.

Still Burning

Some people in Pennsylvania tried to put the fire out. They tried to dig up all the burning seams of coal. They managed to dig up some. But it cost so much money the people finally gave up.

Even the United States **government** couldn't fix the problem. The government said it would cost $663 million to dig up the whole fire. It would cost much less to pay people to move. So the government offered to buy the homes of everyone in town. Most people took the money and moved away. In 1962, there were 1,100 people living in Centralia. By 1998, that number had dropped to 42. Once there had been about 500 buildings in town. By 1998, there were fewer than 30. The rest had caved in or been knocked down.

The Centralia fire is still burning. It has spread through more and more tunnels. There is no sign that the fire will burn out anytime soon. "It's cooking right along, just like it has been for years," said one official in 1998. It will only stop when all the seams of coal have burned up. Until then, it is safe to say that no one will want to move to Centralia, Pennsylvania.

The fire in the mining tunnels burned holes through the earth.

Read and Remember — Finish the Sentence

🔥 Circle the best ending for each sentence.

1. Todd Domboski fell into a _____.
   trap   hole   pool

2. Todd was saved by his _____.
   mother   cousin   dog

3. The fire in Centralia began in a _____.
   school yard   factory   garbage dump

4. The fire was fed by _____.
   trees   coal   oil

5. People in Centralia were paid to _____.
   fight the fire   keep quiet   move out of town

6. No one was able to _____.
   save Eric Wolfgang   put out the fire   leave Centralia

Write About It

🔥 Imagine you live in Centralia, Pennsylvania. Write a letter to a friend explaining why he or she should not move there.

Dear _____ ,

_____

_____

_____

_____

_____

Focus on Vocabulary — Crossword Puzzle

Use the clues to complete the puzzle. Choose from the words in dark print.

officials   Fahrenheit   poisonous   evil   coal

tunnels   government   sinkhole   oxygen   seam

Across
1. harmful
4. what people breathe
7. black rock found in ground
8. scale used for measuring heat
10. a thin layer of rock

Down
2. hole covered by grass
3. very bad
5. people who run a country
6. people in charge
9. pathways built underground

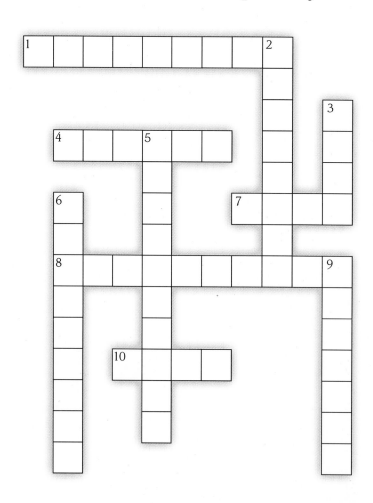

How Fire Starts

Three things must be present for a fire to start. There must be a **fuel**, or something that can burn. **Coal** and wood are kinds of fuel. There also must be **oxygen**, a gas in the air. Finally, there must be enough heat to cause the fuel to catch on fire. Study the diagram below. Circle the answer to each question.

| **Fuel** (something that can burn) | **Oxygen** (a gas in the air) | **Heat** (causes the fuel to start burning) | **Fire** (burning fuel gives off heat and light) |

1. What is one example of a fuel?
   coal   light   heat

2. What is oxygen?
   a type of tree   a spark   a gas in the air

3. What might heat a fuel to its burning point?
   lightning   rain   darkness

4. Once a fire starts, what does it give off?
   wood   coldness   heat and light

A Deadly Surprise

A cloud of steam hung over several villages in southern Mexico. The steam came from a **volcano** called El Chichón. No one paid much attention to this volcano. Steam had been drifting out of it for hundreds of years. Still, in March of 1982 El Chichón seemed to be rumbling more than usual. Some **geologists** decided to check it out. One geologist who decided to go to El Chichón was Salvador Soto.

El Chichón Wakes Up

Soto and other geologists planned to fly to El Chichón at the end of March. But on March 29 the volcano surprised everyone. It **erupted**. Hot gas exploded high into the air. **Ash** and rocks flew everywhere. The burning ash set fire to nearby villages. Roofs caved in. Rocks hit some people on the head. In all, 50 people died. Ash covered the ground for miles around. "There's nothing left on the mountain, only stones and ash," said one man sadly.

Soto and the other geologists were amazed by what had happened. They rushed to southern Mexico. As they neared El Chichón, they found that the air was still full of ash and dust. They had to use a special plane to fly over the volcano. The dust would have **clogged** the engine of any other plane.

"We flew over the volcano and saw strong **activity**," geologist Federico Mooser remembered. That meant the volcano might erupt again. Still, Mooser and Soto did not think people should **panic**.

They didn't think everyone needed to move out of their homes. "We said calm, calm, you shouldn't act so fast," Mooser later explained.

The Village of Francisco León

On Friday, April 2, Mooser and Soto went to visit one of the places nearest the volcano. It was a small village called Francisco León. "We saw for the first time roofs that had caved in, but also many that had not," Mooser said. Most people in the village had run away when the volcano exploded. But 30 or 40 were still there. They didn't want to leave their homes.

The two geologists walked around for about 25 minutes. Then Mooser flew off to meet with some Mexican officials. Salvador Soto stayed behind. He wanted to spend a little more time in Francisco León. Mooser thought a helicopter would bring Soto out later in the day. But the helicopter never showed up. So Soto was left to spend the night in the dusty, ash-covered village.

That evening, Soto sent radio messages out from Francisco León every hour. But the messages stopped at 11 P.M. No one knew why. Perhaps the radio was broken. Mooser hoped that was it. He hoped to be back in touch with Soto the next day.

The Biggest Blast of All

The next day, however, El Chichón began spitting out hot rocks and ash again. Ash blew out about every five minutes. No plane could fly over the volcano now. No plane could get to Francisco León either. Mooser tried to drive his car in. But ash was falling like rain. As it settled, it formed a thick, **dense** layer on the ground. Soon Mooser's car got stuck in the deep ash. He had to spend the night in a village 16 miles from Francisco León and Salvador Soto.

All Saturday night the volcano shot out burning ash. It looked like someone was setting off fireworks inside El Chichón. At 5:20 A.M. on Sunday morning came the biggest blast of all. A huge cloud of ash blew more than five miles into the air. It darkened the sky for 44 hours. **Lava**, or rivers of melted rock, also poured from the volcano. Hot pebbles flew through the air. The villages closest to El Chichón were wiped

Lava poured from the volcano.

out, including Francisco León. Even towns 35 miles away were badly damaged.

Hundreds of people were killed by the **explosion**. Others barely got out alive. "The fire started coming out of the sky," said a man named Guillermo Ruíz. "We didn't know whether to leave or stay. Ash and sand were falling, and rocks came through the roof like bullets."

Federico Mooser was one person who got away safely. He walked ten hours to get away from the spreading lava. But Salvador Soto was not so lucky. He was never seen or heard from again.

It was two weeks before rescue workers could get to the village of Francisco León. They found every building buried in ash. It looked like dump trucks had dumped loads of dusty black sand on each building. Every person who had been in the village was dead.

Geologists around the world were sad to learn of Soto's death. They hoped that in the future they would do a better job of figuring out when volcanoes will erupt. They knew that if they could do that, they could save thousands of lives.

The volcano buried the nearby houses in ash.

Read and Remember — Check the Events

Place a check in front of the three sentences that tell what happened in the story.

_____ **1.** Salvador Soto refused to get near El Chichón.

_____ **2.** Federico Mooser flew to southern Mexico.

_____ **3.** People in Francisco León took pictures of El Chichón.

_____ **4.** Hot rocks and ash began to fly out of El Chichón.

_____ **5.** Guillermo Ruíz saved the life of Federico Mooser.

_____ **6.** Salvador Soto died near El Chichón.

Think About It — Cause and Effect

A **cause** is something that makes something else happen. What happens is called the **effect**. Match each cause with an effect. Write the letter on the correct blank. The first one is done for you.

Cause	Effect
1. A deep layer of ash formed on the ground, so __**d**__	**a.** geologists rushed to southern Mexico.
2. El Chichón began to spit out ash and rocks, so _____	**b.** a special plane was used to fly over the volcano.
3. Most planes could not fly through the dust and ash, so _____	**c.** they told everyone to calm down.
4. Mooser wanted to meet with Mexican officials, so _____	**d.** Mooser's car got stuck.
5. Mooser and Soto did not think people should panic, so _____	**e.** he left Francisco León.

Focus on Vocabulary — Make a Word

Choose a word in dark print to complete each sentence. Write the letters of the word on the blanks. When you are finished, the letters in the circles will tell how Salvador Soto expected to get out of Francisco León.

geologists   **erupted**   **lava**   **explosion**   **ash**

volcano   **dense**   **panic**   **activity**   **clogged**

1. The ground became covered with _____. ⬡ _ _ _

2. Dust would have _____ the engines of the plane. _ _ _ _ _ _ _

3. Hot _____ poured out of the volcano. ⬡ _ _ _ _

4. The big _____ killed many people. _ _ _ _ _ _ _ _ _

5. El Chichón is a _____ in Mexico. _ _ _ _ _ _ _

6. Some _____ rushed to study El Chichón. _ _ _ _ _ _ _ _ _ _

7. Mooser and Soto told people not to _____. ⬡ _ _ _ _

8. The volcano showed strong signs of _____. _ _ _ _ _ _ _ _

9. The layer of ash was very heavy and _____. _ _ _ _ _

10. On Sunday, April 4, El Chichón _____. _ _ _ _ _ _ _

Earth's Layers

When a **volcano** erupts, hot melted rock comes out from deep inside Earth. The Earth is made of three main layers. These are called the **crust**, **mantle**, and **core**. The diagram below shows Earth's layers. Study the diagram. Circle the answer to each question.

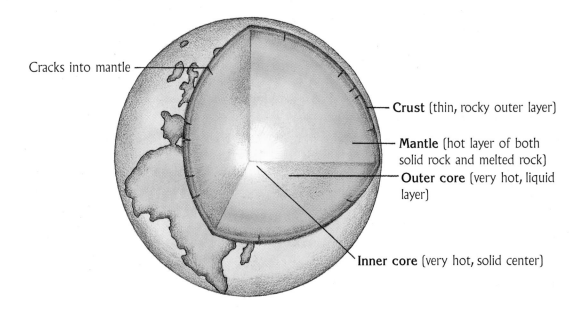

Cracks into mantle

Crust (thin, rocky outer layer)

Mantle (hot layer of both solid rock and melted rock)

Outer core (very hot, liquid layer)

Inner core (very hot, solid center)

1. What is the Earth's thin, outer layer called?

mountains   core   crust

2. What is the mantle made of?

iron   solid and melted rock   ash

3. Which layer is completely solid?

inner core   mantle   outer core

4. From which layer does hot, melted rock come out through cracks in the Earth's crust?

mantle   inner core   outer core

5. What is the outer layer or crust like?

rock   solid   gas

Hit by Lightning

Eleven-year-old Nicky Schneider ran down the soccer field. He headed for the ball, hoping to kick it away from the other team. Just then, rain began to fall on the field in Arlington, Texas. Within a few minutes, Nicky and the other players were soaking wet. Nicky made another run for the ball. But suddenly a flash of lightning **streaked** across the sky. It headed straight for Nicky Schneider on April 7, 1984.

A Blue-White Light

The parents who were watching the game looked on in **horror**. They saw the **bolt** of lightning strike Nicky on the head. For an instant, his whole body was lit by a blue-white light. A huge wave of electricity hit him. It was 100,000 times more powerful than the electricity needed to light a light bulb.

Nicky's body was thrown 12 feet into the air. When he landed, smoke was coming out of his mouth and ears. The tops of his soccer shoes had been blown off his feet. He had burn marks on his head and down his left side. Worst of all, he was not breathing. His heart had stopped beating.

Two women rushed over to where Nicky lay. One was Linda Casagrande. The other was Avril Rush. They both had some **medical** training. Quickly they went to work trying to save Nicky's life.

Again and again Casagrande pushed down on Nicky's chest. She tried to get his heart to start pumping. Rush blew air into his mouth. She tried to

Linda Casagrande

get fresh oxygen to his **lungs** and brain.

As they worked, Nicky's mother ran over. "He's dead," she cried when she saw her son. Casagrande and Rush feared Bonnie Schneider was right. But they didn't give up. They kept working as hard as they could.

Barely Alive

After twelve minutes, an ambulance came. Nicky was rushed to the hospital. On the way, his heart started to beat again. It was a slow, weak beat. But at least it showed that Nicky was alive. At the hospital, the beating grew stronger. Still, Nicky was not awake. He could not breathe on his own. Doctors hooked him up to a special machine. It pumped air into his lungs.

The machine helped Nicky breathe for days. Tests showed a lot of **swelling** deep in his brain. Doctors didn't know if Nicky would ever wake up. Even if he did, they didn't know how much brain damage he

The lightning burned Nicky's clothing and made his shoes fly off.

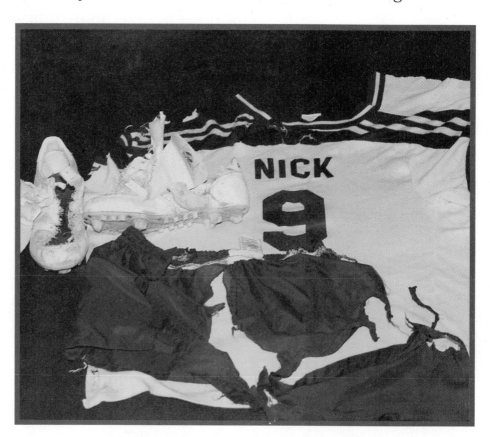

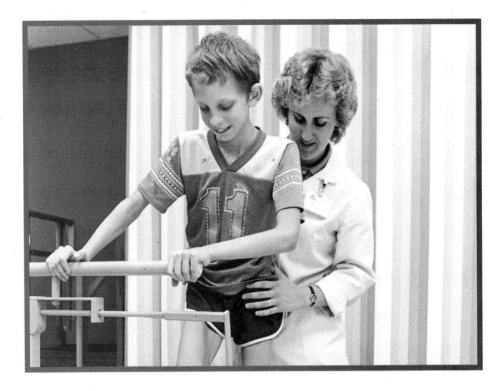

Nicky worked hard to get better after the accident.

Lightning

would have. They had never seen a case like his before. Most people who are directly hit by lightning are killed instantly.

Dr. Lowell Stanley thought he knew why Nicky had **survived**. He thought it was because of the rain. Nicky's body had been covered with a thin coat of rain when the lightning struck him. So some of the electricity would have flowed along this coating. It could have passed down into the ground without all of it entering his body. In fact, the thin coating kept Nicky's body from getting badly burned.

Most of the electricity did enter Nicky's body. It flowed from his chest to his legs. It burned his lungs and hurt his heart. Without the help from Casagrande and Rush, Nicky would have died within a few minutes. They had worked together to keep blood and oxygen moving through Nicky's body.

Getting Better

Thirteen days after he entered the hospital, Nicky Schneider woke up. He tried to speak. But he couldn't say any words. He could only make a few weak sounds. He couldn't walk. He couldn't sit up. He tried to take a drink of orange juice. But the juice ran down his chin.

The doctors knew what this meant. The lightning had killed many **cells** in one part of the brain. These brain cells had controlled much of Nicky's body **movements**. Doctors hoped that other brain cells would take over. These other cells would have to learn new jobs. They would have to learn to control the movements of Nicky's body.

For weeks, doctors and nurses worked with Nicky. They taught him how to move his mouth to form words. They helped him bend his arms and legs. It was hard work. But Nicky made great **progress**. Finally he was able to feed himself again. He could say words clearly. After a month, he began taking steps on his own. By summer he could ride his bike and tie his own shoes.

It was a long time before Nicky could run without pain. The tops of his feet had been badly burned by the lightning. But in time, the burns healed. About a year later, Nicky started playing soccer again. That's when everyone knew he really was going to be okay.

Nicky Schneider will never forget how lightning affected his life.

Read and Remember — Choose the Answer

Draw a circle around the correct answer.

1. What sport was Nicky Schneider playing?

   football   soccer   baseball

2. Where was Nicky taken after he was hit by lightning?

   to the hospital   to his house   to his father's shop

3. What was on Nicky's body when he was hit?

   a metal whistle   rubber boots   a coating of water

4. How long did it take Nicky to wake up?

   thirteen minutes   thirteen hours   thirteen days

5. What did doctors and nurses have to teach Nicky to do?

   cough   blink his eyes   bend his arms

Write About It

Imagine you are Nicky Schneider's brother or sister. Write a paragraph describing what it is like to live with Nicky as he works to get better.

_____

_____

_____

_____

_____

_____

43

Focus on Vocabulary — Finish Up

Choose the correct word in dark print to complete each sentence.

bolt	**streaked**	**horror**	**progress**	**cells**
movements	**survived**	**lungs**	**medical**	**swelling**

1. The moves that a person makes with his or her body are _____.

2. All living things are made up of _____.

3. To have lived through something is to have _____.

4. A flash of lightning is called a lightning _____.

5. The _____ are a part of the body used for breathing.

6. To get closer to a goal is to make _____.

7. If something is _____ it has to do with medicine.

8. Something that moved very fast has _____.

9. A _____ means growth in size.

10. A feeling of great fear is _____.

Lightning Strikes

Lightning can strike metal and other good **conductors**. Lightning does not strike poor conductors. Study the information below about conductors. Place a check (✔) under *Likely* or *Not Likely* to show whether lightning might strike each object.

Would lightning directly strike it?	Likely	Not Likely
1. metal weather vane	_____	_____
2. rubber tire	_____	_____
3. metal pitch fork	_____	_____
4. metal roof	_____	_____
5. window	_____	_____
6. metal barbed-wire fence	_____	_____

Buried in the Night

Something strange was happening in the South American town of Armero, Colombia. At 5:30 P.M. on November 13, 1985, ash began to float down from the sky. The air began to smell strange, too. It smelled like rotten eggs.

The ash came from Nevado del Ruiz, a volcano about 30 miles away. The smell came from there, too. Many people wondered if the volcano was getting ready to erupt. But officials in Armero said there was no great danger. These officials were wrong.

Warning Signs

Sixteen-year-old Slaye Molina lived in Armero. She listened to radio **announcers** telling everyone to stay calm. The announcers believed there was no danger. Slaye **assumed** they were right. So that night she and her family settled down to watch TV. Then they went to bed.

Meanwhile, Nevado del Ruiz was getting ready to explode. For months there had been warning signs. In 1984, after hundreds of years of silence, the volcano had begun to rumble. Deep inside the earth, a thick soup of melted rocks was bubbling upward. This red-hot **liquid** was called **magma**.

Then on September 11, 1985, small amounts of hot ash and rocks flew out of the volcano. This mixed with ice and snow on top of the 17,680-foot volcano. It made a kind of hot mud called **lahar**. The mud flowed down the mountain. But it didn't kill anyone. It didn't reach Armero or any other nearby towns. So most people didn't worry about it.

A large wall of mud moved through the town.

Scientists were worried that the volcano would erupt soon.

Scientists, however, were worried. They thought Nevado del Ruiz was getting ready for a big blast. They even drew up a map of towns that might be in danger. Armero was on the map.

Most people paid little attention. After all, the scientists couldn't say when the volcano would erupt. People thought it would be years in the future. So they made no plans to leave their homes.

Sadly, the scientists were right. On the night of November 13, Nevado del Ruiz erupted. Hot gas, ash, and rocks flew out of the volcano. It wasn't a huge **eruption**. In fact, it was quite small. It melted only a small amount of the ice and snow on top of the volcano.

Still, that was more than enough. The melting ice and snow caused a huge flood of lahar. The hot mud flowed down the mountain. It picked up everything in its path. By the time it got to Armero, it had turned into a wall of water, dirt, ash, and rocks. The moving wall of mud gained speed as it flowed down the mountain. It grew bigger and bigger. As it got close to Armero, it was more than 10 feet high. That made it higher than a basketball hoop. Soon this wall of water, dirt, ash, and rocks would hit the town.

Finding Higher Ground

The people of Armero did not see Nevado del Ruiz erupt. It had been raining earlier in the evening and storm clouds still covered the top of the volcano. So the people did not see the hot lahar sweeping toward them. The radio continued to play happy music. At 11:35 P.M. the huge wall of steaming mud reached the town. Slaye Molina said it looked "like a cloud." By that time, people were screaming in fear. To them, it looked as if the world was coming to an end.

Slaye saw a neighbor's house **collapse** as the lahar hit it. Slaye ran outside. A friend grabbed her hand and pulled her toward a nearby hill. Luckily, they made it to higher ground before the hot mud caught them. "When we reached the hill," Slaye later said, "We saw Armero disappear in 15 minutes."

One Happy Ending

After the lahar cooled, rescue workers began digging through it to find any people still alive. It was sad work. But one happy story came out of

Rescue workers rushed to help people after the eruption.

the **tragedy**. Twenty-four days after the volcano blew, a man named Alberto Nunez walked up the mountain. He wanted to see if there was anything left of his house. As he neared Armero, he saw a neighbor's house half buried in mud. He was surprised to see smoke rising from the chimney.

Nunez looked inside. What he saw amazed him even more. Elvira Echeverry, age 66, was still alive inside the house. She had never left. Somehow most of the lahar had flowed around Echeverry's house, leaving it standing. Echeverry had lit a fire to keep the flies out of her house. Then she had simply waited for help to come.

By the time Nunez found her, she had eaten all the food that she had in the house. She just had a little muddy water left to drink. She was sharing this with her dog.

Elvira Echeverry and Slaye Molina survived the eruption. But many others were not so lucky. In all, the volcano took the lives of more than 23,000 people. It was one of the worst **natural disasters** in South America's history.

The eruption wiped out the town of Armero.

Read and Remember — Finish the Sentence

Circle the best ending for each sentence.

1. The air around Nevado del Ruiz smelled like _____.
   rotten eggs   soap   bacon frying

2. Scientists thought the volcano would _____.
   slowly crumble   become quiet   explode

3. As hot mud flowed toward her house, Slaye Molina ran _____.
   to a church   up a hill   inside

4. The town of Armero was _____.
   not harmed   wiped out   hit by high winds

5. Weeks after the explosion, Alberto Nunez walked _____.
   up the mountain   into the volcano   to the ocean

6. When the volcano exploded, Elvira Echeverry stayed _____.
   in Mexico   with Slaye Molina   in her house

Think About It — Find the Sequence

_____ 1. Radio announcers told people to stay calm.

___1___ 2. Ash began to float down from the sky.

_____ 3. Alberto Nunez found Elvira Echeverry still alive.

_____ 4. Slaye Molina saw a neighbor's house collapse.

_____ 5. Alberto Nunez saw smoke coming from the chimney of a house half buried in mud.

Focus on Vocabulary — Match Up

Match each word with its meaning. Darken the circle beside the correct answer.

1. announcers
- ○ workers
- ○ officials
- ○ people who tell news

2. assumed
- ○ believed
- ○ did not trust
- ○ told people what to do

3. liquid
- ○ something that can be poured
- ○ rock
- ○ gas

4. magma
- ○ beautiful scene
- ○ purple berry
- ○ melted rocks

5. lahar
- ○ hot mud
- ○ a thin coating
- ○ mix of ice and snow

6. scientists
- ○ officers
- ○ people who study sciences
- ○ builders

7. eruption
- ○ bursting out
- ○ discovery
- ○ looking for clues

8. collapse
- ○ come together
- ○ fall apart
- ○ stand still

9. tragedy
- ○ funny event
- ○ sad event
- ○ true story

10. natural disasters
- ○ terrible acts of nature
- ○ changes
- ○ reports

Inside a Volcano

A **volcano** is a hole on Earth's rocky outer layer. **Magma,** made up of melted rock and hot gas, comes out of the hole. Once magma leaves the volcano, it hardens into rock. The diagram below shows the parts of a volcano. Study the diagram. Circle the answer to complete each sentence.

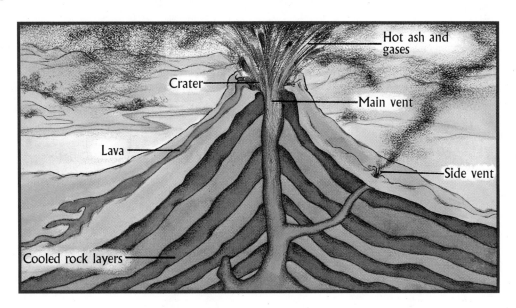

1. The bowl-shaped top of a volcano is the _____.

    lava   magma   crater

2. An opening that allows magma to come out is called a _____.

    gas   vent   lava

3. Once hot magma leaves the volcano, it is called _____.

    lava   crater   hard rock

4. A volcano might send _____ into the air.

    hot ash and gases   vents   lightning sparks

5. Lava hardens into _____.

    gases   rock   magma

No Place to Hide

alif Tervo had been climbing mountains for almost 20 years. One of his favorites was California's Mount Whitney. At 14,494 feet, it is one of the highest mountains in the United States. Tervo had already climbed Mount Whitney ten times. But on July 14, 1990, he headed up it again. This time he went with two friends, James and Glen MacLeod. The trip started out like all the others. But this time Tervo was lucky to get back down alive.

A Stone Hut

The weather was fine as the three men started toward the top. "It was a beautiful day, sunny and about 80 **degrees** out," Tervo remembered. But that soon changed. As the day went on, a weather **front** moved in. Cold air began to mix with the warm air. Clouds developed. By afternoon it was raining.

"When it started raining, our first thought was to get dry," James MacLeod said. So the three men looked around for shelter. By this time, they were right near the top of the mountain. They saw an old stone hut. It had been built for **astronomers** years earlier. Astronomers had studied the stars from this hut. Tervo and the MacLeods ran into it. Ten other hikers did the same thing. As they gathered inside, lightning started to shoot across the sky.

For the next half hour the group waited for the storm to pass. During that time, Calif Tervo began to wonder if they had picked a safe spot. After all, the hut had a metal roof. Tervo knew lightning was

attracted to metal. So he asked the other hikers what they thought.

The group talked about it for a few minutes. They knew many people had used the hut for shelter over the years. No one had ever been hurt in it. So they figured the hut must be "**grounded**." That would mean it had a metal pole called a **lightning rod**. The rod would run from the roof straight into the ground. Any lightning that hit the hut would run along this pole. It would shoot deep into the ground. Then it would be **absorbed** by the earth. It would not harm anyone.

Lightning Strikes

The old hut did not have a lightning rod. It was not grounded. If lightning struck the hut, harmful amounts of electricity could pass through everyone who was inside.

At 3:30 p.m., that's just what happened. A huge bolt of lightning hit the metal roof. "There was a huge explosion inside," said Tervo. "There were buzzes and crackling. It was the sound of electricity running

Lightning storms can occur just about anywhere, including on mountains.

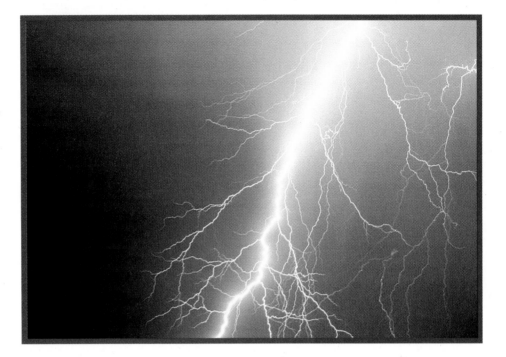

Lightning is very powerful.

everywhere. You could smell burning clothes and burning skin. I thought I was dead."

All 13 hikers were hit. But some were hit harder than others. Calif Tervo fell down. He struck his head on the floor and passed out. James MacLeod was also knocked out. So was hiker Matthew Nordbrook. Tervo soon woke up. But MacLeod and Nordbrook did not. The lightning had stopped their hearts.

MacLeod and Nordbrook

When Tervo first woke up, he couldn't move. His legs were **numb**. He watched the other hikers rushing to help MacLeod and Nordbrook. They pushed down on the chests of both men, hoping to get the hearts pumping again.

For James MacLeod, it worked. After 20 minutes he woke up. He was in a lot of pain. He had a large burn on his right shoulder. That was where he had been leaning against the wall. It was where lightning had entered his body.

MacLeod also had many smaller burns on his body. That was where the lightning had shot out of him. In each of these spots, the lightning had burned a hole right through his clothing. It had even melted his heavy ski jacket. "It's **unbelievable** what it did to me," he said. "It's so scary to think about how it just went right through me."

By the time James MacLeod woke up, Tervo felt better. He and another hiker offered to hurry down the mountain to get help. Everyone else stayed in the hut to work on Nordbrook.

Tervo didn't think it would be hard to get down the mountain. "I'd made the climb up with no trouble," he said. "So I thought going down would be easy." But his legs were still quite numb. He couldn't move very fast. As he **staggered** down, the other hiker raced on ahead.

It took hours to get help. Finally, at 8:30 P.M., rescue workers reached the stone hut. They rushed Nordbrook to the hospital. But nothing could be done to save him. He was already dead.

The other hikers were very upset by Nordbrook's death. But they were thankful to be alive. "It could have been all thirteen of us that didn't make it," said Glen MacLeod. "We were very lucky."

The hikers waited to be rescued from Mount Whitney.

Read and Remember — Check the Events

Place a check in front of the three sentences that tell what happened in the story.

_____ **1.** Calif Tervo climbed up Mount Whitney.

_____ **2.** Thirteen hikers got caught in a big snowstorm.

_____ **3.** Wind blew the lightning rod off a hut on Mount Whitney.

_____ **4.** Lightning struck a hut where hikers had gathered.

_____ **5.** James MacLeod refused to leave his friend on the mountain.

_____ **6.** Matthew Nordbrook was killed by lightning.

Write About It

Write a paragraph telling whether or not you think the stone hut on Mount Whitney should be open to hikers.

_____

_____

_____

_____

_____

_____

_____

_____

_____

Focus on Vocabulary — Crossword Puzzle

Use the clues to complete the puzzle. Choose from the words in dark print.

staggered   **degrees**   **front**   **astronomers**

unbelievable   **attracted**   **numb**   **absorbed**

lightning rod   **grounded**

Across

1. soaked up
3. drawn toward
5. metal pole that runs into the ground
7. having lost all feeling
9. walked with great trouble

Down

1. people who study stars
2. hard to believe
4. where cold and warm air meet
6. protected from lightning
8. units of measure

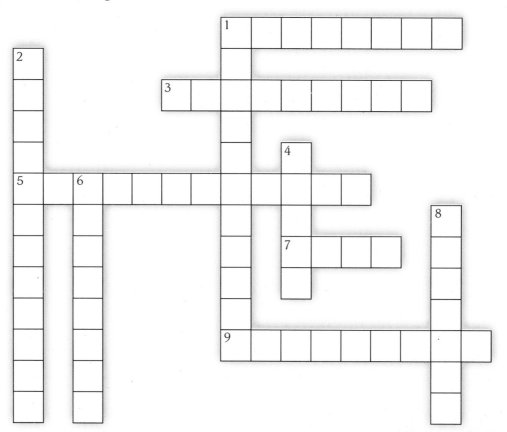

Weather Map

A **weather map** shows what kind of weather to expect in an area. The map below shows one day's weather in the United States. The **map key** explains what the symbols or colors on the map mean. Study the map. Circle the answer to each question.

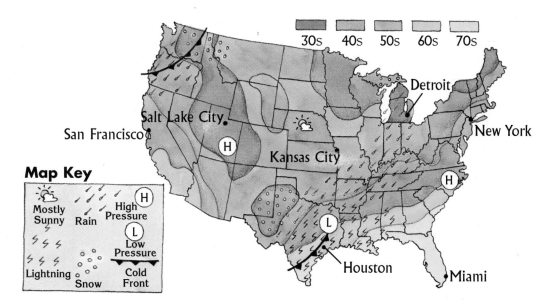

1. Which is the symbol for lightning?

2. What color is used to show a temperature of 35°F?
   dark green   blue   yellow

3. What is the weather like in Detroit?
   sunny   rainy   snowy

4. Which city should expect thunderstorms with lightning?
   Houston   New York   Miami

5. Which city has the same temperature as Salt Lake City?
   Detroit   San Francisco   Houston

Escape from a Volcano

ount Pinatubo had been quiet for more than 600 years. Then, on April 2, 1991, this volcano in the Philippines began to wake up. A tiny eruption sent steam and a bit of ash into the air. This by itself was no trouble. But it was a bad sign of things to come.

The tiny blast showed that Mount Pinatubo was no longer **dormant**. It might soon erupt in a bigger way that could cause terrible damage. Thousands of people lived near the volcano. If it blew up, they might all die.

Getting It Right

Scientists knew they had to act and act fast. They remembered what had happened with other volcanoes. In 1982 Mexico's El Chichón had started to rumble. No one paid any attention until it was too late. Hundreds of people died when that volcano exploded. An even bigger tragedy had taken place in Colombia in 1985. There the Nevado del Ruiz volcano had given warning signs. Scientists knew the volcano might explode. But they couldn't **predict** when. More than 23,000 people died when Nevado del Ruiz suddenly erupted.

This time scientists were determined to do a better job. They began to watch Mount Pinatubo very closely. On April 5, they picked up important sounds. They heard the earth shifting deep below the volcano's **surface**. Over the next two months, these sounds continued. Scientists knew steam and magma were forcing their way toward the surface. It was like a balloon being pumped with too much air. Mount Pinatubo was getting ready to pop.

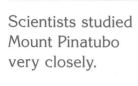
Scientists studied Mount Pinatubo very closely.

By early June, the sounds were close to the surface. There was no question now. The volcano was about to erupt. Scientists could tell that it wouldn't be a small eruption. It would be one of the biggest the world had ever seen. Clearly, it was time to sound an alarm. The lives of millions of people were at **stake**.

Just in Time

Quickly the scientists turned to Philippine officials. They **convinced** the officials that the danger was real. Over the next few days, the officials moved one million people out of their homes.

The officials acted just in time. On June 12, Mount Pinatubo exploded. It sent up a cloud of steam and ash that could be seen 60 miles away. This cloud shot up 10 miles into the sky. One writer said the blast was "like an **atomic bomb**."

The eruption wiped out every village within seven miles of the volcano. More than 70,000 people lived in these villages. Their homes were completely buried in ash and mud. Luckily, the people themselves were saved. They were among those who had been sent to safer ground.

Ash and Mud

The volcano also damaged places farther away. The city of Angeles was about ten miles from Mount Pinatubo. About 280,000 people lived there. The volcano sent eight inches of ash and sand pouring down on this city. To make things worse, a storm brought heavy rains. The rain mixed with ash to **create** rivers of mud. Many homes collapsed under the weight of the ash. Others were washed away in **mudslides**.

Solidad Santiago was one whose home collapsed. She and her family got out just in time. But everything they owned was lost. "We have nothing except the clothes we are wearing," she said.

Everything nearby was covered in heavy ash.

More than 700,000 people lost their homes when the volcano erupted.

The ash made it hard to breathe.

Angelo Luciano's house also collapsed. He and his wife were trapped inside. "Our neighbors dug into the **rubble** and saved us," Luciano said. "We are very lucky to be alive."

Romayo Garcia felt the same way. The ash caused the roof of his house collapse. He and his family walked 20 miles to get away from the falling ash. "We have lost everything," he said. "But still I am happy, happy to be here."

Mount Pinatubo did not stop erupting after June 12. For the next two months it continued to send out ash and steam. In addition, so much ash covered the ground that every rain brought more mudslides.

In the end, the volcano killed 847 people. Some were people who refused to leave their homes. Others didn't hear the warnings. Many others got caught in mudslides. Beyond that, more than 700,000 people lost their homes. The volcano did a lot of damage. Still, the scientists were **satisfied** with their work. They had correctly predicted the volcano's eruption. As scientist Dan Miller said, "Tens of thousands of lives were saved."

Read and Remember — Choose the Answer

Draw a circle around the correct answer.

1. Where is Mount Pinatubo found?

Mexico   Colombia   Philippines

2. What was shifting deep below the volcano's surface?

the earth   water   ice

3. What did scientists want people near the volcano to do?

gather in schools   move out   lock their doors

4. When Mount Pinatubo exploded, what was sent into the air?

ash and steam   large rocks   lava

5. What did 700,000 people lose?

their homes   their families   their lives

Think About It — Fact or Opinion

A **fact** is a true statement. An **opinion** is a statement that tells what a person thinks. Write **F** beside each statement that is a fact. Write **O** beside each statement that is an opinion.

_____ **1.** Every village within 7 miles of the volcano was wiped out.

_____ **2.** Ash and dust fell on the city of Angeles.

_____ **3.** People should always listen to scientists.

_____ **4.** Nothing is scarier than a volcano that is about to erupt.

_____ **5.** The roof of Romayo Garcia's house collapsed.

_____ **6.** Officials moved one million people out of their homes.

Focus on Vocabulary — Finish the Paragraphs

Use the words in dark print to complete the paragraphs. Reread the paragraphs to be sure they make sense.

convinced	**stake**	**create**	**rubble**	**satisfied**
mudslides	**surface**	**predict**	**dormant**	**atomic bomb**

In the spring of 1991, scientists became **(1)**_____ that Mount Pinatubo was going to erupt. The volcano had been **(2)**_____ for more than 600 years. But now the earth was shifting far below the **(3)**_____ of the volcano. Scientists hoped to **(4)**_____ exactly when Mount Pinatubo would erupt. They knew that the lives of thousands of people were at **(5)**_____.

In early June, a million people were moved away from the volcano. On June 12, the big explosion came. It sounded like an **(6)**_____. Soon rain fell and mixed with the ash to **(7)**_____ rivers of mud. This led to **(8)**_____. Homes and buildings collapsed. People such as Angelo Luciano were lucky to escape from the **(9)**_____. Still, scientists were **(10)**_____ with their work. They had saved the lives of many people.

The Ring of Fire

Volcanoes often occur along moving **plates**. These plates are large pieces of Earth's rocky **surface**. Most volcanoes are along the Pacific Ocean. This area is called the Ring of Fire. Study the map of the Ring of Fire below. Write the answer to each question.

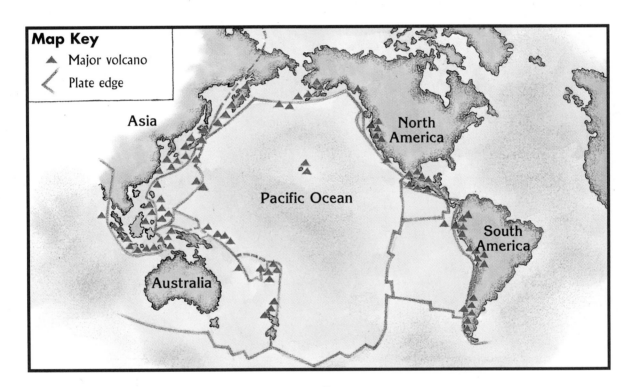

Map Key
▲ Major volcano
‹ Plate edge

Asia

North America

Pacific Ocean

South America

Australia

1. Around what ocean are the volcanoes? _____

2. What are the names of the four land areas along the Ring of Fire? _____

3. What are the large pieces of Earth's surface called? _____

4. Why is the area called the Ring of Fire? _____

_____

5. Is there an edge of a plate along South America? _____

_____

Wind and Fire

On October 27, 1993, a man named Andres Huang was camping out among some trees. He was in Angeles National Forest in southern California. It was a cold night. To stay warm, Huang started a small fire. He didn't mean to set fire to the **surrounding** land. But that's what happened. An **ember** from his campfire landed in the brush. The dry brush quickly burst into flames. Within hours, the fire was burning out of control.

Hot and Dry

The out-of-control campfire was just one of many that broke out that day. Fires are often a problem in southern California in the fall. That's because it almost never rains from May to October. The land becomes very dry.

There is another reason as well. That is the winds. Southern California often gets hit by powerful winds, known as Santa Ana winds. These winds are different from other winds. They are made up of very hot air. These winds help to dry up any **moisture** still in the ground. Worse, these **gusts** are so strong that they can turn a small flame into a roaring fire within minutes.

Santa Ana winds begin in Nevada and Utah. They move west through mountains called the Sierra Nevada. Along the way, the winds have to pass through some narrow **canyons**. One is the Santa Ana Canyon. That's where the Santa Ana winds get their name.

The canyons act as **funnels**. They squeeze the air as the winds pass through. This adds speed as well as heat to the winds.

By the time the winds reach California, they are blowing 35 to 40 miles an hour. Sometimes they hit speeds of 100 miles an hour. By this time, too, the winds are very hot. They can be 25 degrees warmer than they were when they first began in Nevada and Utah.

Fighting Fire

Al Miller knew all about the Santa Ana winds. In fact, he named his cat "Santa Ana Winds". Miller lived with his wife and cat just outside Laguna Beach, California. Miller wasn't home when the fires began spreading toward his house. But his wife was. Quickly she packed up some things and left.

Al Miller was **relieved** that his wife had gotten out of the house safely. But he was upset to learn that

Fires are often a problem in southern California in the fall.

she had forgotten his cat. Miller couldn't bear to think of losing his cat. So he decided to go back and look for her.

He tried to drive back but police had closed the road. So Miller set out on foot. He walked the two miles to his home. By then, the flames were just a few feet away. Miller looked around in panic. Finally he saw his cat. She was right near the house, crying in fear. Miller grabbed her and rushed off as the fire took over his house.

Not far away, Dr. Carlos Ruiz and his wife and son were busy trying to save their home in Pasadena, California. The Ruizes cut down nine trees near their house. That way the fire couldn't jump from the trees to the house. Fewer trees meant less fuel for the fire. The Ruizes also used a garden hose to wet down the roof. That way no embers could set fire to it. All night the family kept watch. By morning, the danger was over. They had taken a huge chance. But it had paid off. The fire never reached their house.

Other people weren't so lucky. Jane Arvizu lost her whole house to the flames. The blaze was so strong that it even burned the toilet. "You don't realize what fire does to things," she said.

One Hundred Fires

Firefighters did their best to battle the flames. But it wasn't easy. There were far too many fires. Within two days, about one hundred fires broke out. Fanned by the Santa Ana winds, the fires' flames shot up to 70 feet in the air.

The firefighters had another problem, as well. They didn't have nearly enough water. So little rain had fallen that the water **supply** was very low. Some fire **hydrants** ran dry. In one case, firefighters pumped water from a swimming pool to try to save homes.

In all, the fires burned nearly 700 homes and other buildings to the ground. The sky was black with smoke. This smoke could be seen for miles. It was even spotted by **astronauts** 172 miles above Earth.

In the end, the Santa Ana winds and the fires left 25,000 people without homes. But there was some good news. Even though the many fires did a lot of damage, they didn't kill a single person.

The fires burned many homes and other buildings to the ground.

Read and Remember — Finish the Sentence

Circle the best ending for each sentence.

1. Santa Ana winds begin in _____.

Mexico   Nevada and Utah   Montana and Idaho

2. Santa Ana winds are made up of _____.

very hot air   smoke and water   very wet air

3. The Santa Ana winds helped spread _____.

disease   fires   rain

4. Dr. Carlos Ruiz worked all night to save his _____.

hospital   house   cat

5. In 1993 the Santa Ana winds killed _____.

no one   twenty people   more than one hundred people

Write About It

Imagine the Santa Ana winds are pushing flames in the direction of your house. Write a paragraph telling what you would do.

Focus on Vocabulary — Finish Up

Choose the correct word in dark print to complete each sentence.

moisture	**gusts**	**surrounding**	**funnels**	**hydrants**
astronauts	**ember**	**canyons**	**relieved**	**supply**

1. To be freed from worry is to be _____.

2. Water pipes that stick out of the ground and are used by firefighters are called _____.

3. People trained to fly through outer space are _____.

4. Wetness in the air is _____.

5. Strong, sudden bursts of wind are _____.

6. Objects called _____ direct something from a large area through a small area.

7. To be circling on all sides is to be _____.

8. A small piece of wood still glowing with fire is an _____.

9. A _____ is the amount of something that is needed.

10. Deep valleys with high rocky walls are _____.

What Causes Wind?

Air warmed by the sun is lighter than cool air, so the warm air rises. Then cool air rushes in to take the warm air's place. This movement of air makes wind. Study the diagram. Write the answer to each question.

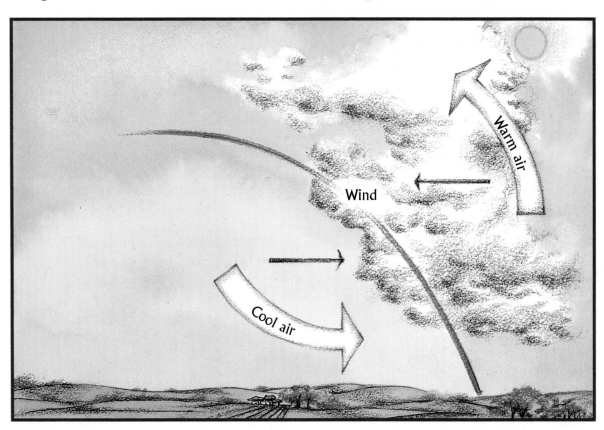

1. What warms the air? _____

_____

2. Which is lighter—warm air or cool air? _____

3. What moves in to replace warm air as it rises? _____

4. What is formed by the movement of air? _____

5. How do you think wind from a fire is similar to wind caused by the sun's heat? _____

_____

Firefighters in Danger

onnie Holtby loved being a firefighter. At age 21, she was the youngest member of the Prineville Hotshot crew. This special group of highly-trained firefighters lived in Prineville, Oregon. But they traveled all over the country. Holtby and her fellow Hotshots spent their days fighting **wildfires**. It took special **courage** to do the job. Every day the Hotshots faced deadly fires that no one else could handle. They knew how to fight dangerous blazes. But near Glenwood Springs, Colorado, on July 6, 1994, they faced a fire that proved too strong even for them.

The Wind Picks Up

The fire started on July 3, 1994. It happened when lightning struck a tree on Storm King Mountain in Colorado. Lightning often starts forest fires. That is because fire needs three things to burn. It needs oxygen, fuel, and heat. Oxygen is found in the air. Trees make good fuel. Lightning makes the heat. A bolt of lightning is very hot. So when it hits a tree, a fire can be started.

By July 6 the forest fire on Storm King Mountain was burning strong. It was ready to burn for a long time. The fire had covered 50 **acres**. That was an area about the size of five city blocks. To the people in Glenwood Springs, the fire looked pretty scary. But to the Prineville Hotshots, it seemed quite ordinary. Hotshot Tom Rambo said, "Our crew goes to so many fires, it seemed like business as usual."

Early on the morning of July 6, the 20 Prineville Hotshots headed up Storm King Mountain. They joined 32 firefighters who were already on the job. As always,

Bonnie Holtby loved being a firefighter.

the Hotshots carried shovels and saws. They planned to cut away a wide strip of brush and trees. That would form a **firebreak**. When the fire reached the strip, it would find nothing to burn. So the fire would die.

The Hotshots split into two groups. Bonnie Holtby's group went down over the side of a **ridge**. Later, Tom Rambo's group moved higher up the mountain. The 32 other firefighters worked nearby.

For hours all 52 men and women cut trees and carried them away. They dug up grass and brush, leaving nothing but dirt. There was very little wind, so the fire was not moving fast. The firefighters were making good progress.

But around 3:30 P.M., the wind suddenly picked up. All at once it started blowing at 50 miles per hour. Hotshot Louie Navarro said, "I've never seen anything like it."

Smoke and Heat

Within seconds, the fire began to surround the firefighters. It moved across the bottom of the **slope** where they were working. "The flames were **incredibly** fast," said Navarro.

The firefighters knew they were in trouble. They had never seen a fire get out of control so quickly. The flames were now whipping along the bottom and sides of the slope. The only place left to run was straight up the mountain.

Most of the firefighters began to run as fast as they could. But it wasn't easy. They couldn't see where they were going. Smoke filled the air. The heat was very strong. Tom Rambo said it "was like standing on the surface of the sun and trying to run some place cool."

Rambo and Navarro were lucky. They were higher up the mountain. So they were able to outrun the flames. Still, some of the people in their group barely made it. Kim Valentine staggered on for as long as she could. But the smoke and heat were too much for her. She collapsed. Fellow Hotshot Bryan Scholz saw her lying on the ground. He quickly helped her up and dragged her along with him. Somehow he got them both to safety.

Not All Survive

Bonnie Holtby's group was in worse shape. They were farther down the mountain and in the fire's path.

Firefighters couldn't stop the fire from spreading up the mountain.

It swept over them with great speed. In less than two minutes the fire had moved from the bottom of the ridge to the top. Some of the firefighters stopped and pulled out their safety blankets. They used these blankets because they were **fireproof**. The blankets were made of **aluminum**. The firefighters thought the aluminum material would keep the fire away. The blankets fit into a pocket but opened to the size of a small tent. By lying under them, some firefighters hoped to live through the fire.

The aluminum blankets did save some people. Nine firefighters were later found alive under them. But for others, the blankets were not enough. They died while wrapped up in them.

In all, 14 firefighters died on that day. Nine of them were Prineville Hotshots. Bonnie Holtby was among the dead. She was the last firefighter in her group coming up the mountain. She was just one minute from the top of the ridge. But the fire had moved faster than Bonnie Holtby.

The Holtby family was deeply saddened by the tragedy. But they knew Holtby had loved being a Hotshot. "I think she saw it as a **challenge**," said her father. "She died doing what she wanted to do."

The fire burned acres and acres of forest on Storm King Mountain.

Read and Remember — Check the Events

Place a check in front of the three sentences that tell what happened in the story.

_____ **1.** Firefighters were sent to fight the blaze on Storm King Mountain.

_____ **2.** Bonnie Holtby forgot to bring all of her equipment with her.

_____ **3.** Some of the firefighters left work early.

_____ **4.** Louie Navarro was able to run ahead of the fire.

_____ **5.** Bonnie Holtby and 13 others died on Storm King Mountain.

_____ **6.** Police officers were called in to help put out the fire.

Think About It — Drawing Conclusions

Write one or more sentences to answer each question.

1. Why do you think the Hotshots were sent to fight the fire?

_____

2. Why do you think the Hotshots split into two groups?

_____

3. What made the fire spread so quickly? _____

_____

4. Why did Bryan Scholz stop to help Kim Valentine? _____

_____

5. Why did the firefighters run away from the flames? _____

_____

Focus on Vocabulary — Find the Meaning

Read each sentence. Circle the best meaning for the word in dark print.

1. The Hotshots knew how to fight **wildfires**.

fires out of control small fires summer fires

2. It took **courage** to do the job.

special training bravery anger

3. The fire had covered 50 **acres**.

hillsides way of measuring land pieces of wood

4. The firefighters wanted to make a **firebreak**.

water for fires fire explosion cleared strip of land

5. The group went over the **ridge**.

a raised strip of land small river steep wall of rock

6. Fire moved across the bottom of the **slope**.

slanted ground rocky field winding dirt road

7. The fire moved **incredibly** fast.

not a surprise along the ground hard to believe

8. The blankets were **fireproof**.

very hot thin and wet not able to burn

9. The blankets were made of **aluminum**.

a light, soft metal a kind of plastic water and dirt

10. Bonnie Holtby loved the **challenge** of being a Hotshot.

pay something hard to do making new friends

How Lightning Occurs

Lightning causes many fires. It occurs because there is a pull between objects that have opposite charges (+ or –). During a lightning storm, opposite charges build up in clouds. Study the diagram. Write the answer to each question.

1. Does the top of the cloud have a + charge or a – charge? _____

2. What charge does the top of the tree have? _____

3. What kind of charge does lightning flow to when it begins at the bottom of the cloud? _____

   _____

4. Could lightning occur between the top of the cloud and the top of the tree? _____

5. What charge does the bottom of the cloud have? _____

   _____

Nature's Fire

he news shocked South Africans. Wild grass fires were **destroying** Kruger National Park. Lightning started these fires in late September 1996. By October 2, the fires were burning out of control. Reports said thousands of animals would burn to death. The park's trees would go up in flames. "This is the worst fire we've had since 1955," said Chris van der Linde, a park official. Most South Africans wanted the fires put out right away. But nothing was being done. Were park officials just going to let the fires burn?

On Fire

Kruger National Park, which was set up in 1926, is huge. The park covers more than 7,000 square miles. That makes it the size of Massachusetts or half the size of Switzerland.

The park is a special place. There are more types of **wildlife** there than most other parks in the world. Kruger National Park has 147 different kinds of animals. It has 510 different kinds of birds. The park also has many kinds of trees, bushes, and flowers. All this makes it a great place to visit. About 700,000 people go to the park each year.

But in 1996, people feared the wildfires would ruin the park. They feared the animals' **habitat** would be destroyed. Strong winds were helping to spread the hot flames. As much as 20 **percent** of the park was on fire. In some places, many small fires had joined together. They turned into roaring walls of flames as high as 30 feet. Usually the roads formed **natural** firebreaks. But this time the flames were so high

Cheetah at Kruger National Park

they leaped right across the roads. New fires then started on the other side.

There was a reason why the fires were so strong. The park had just gone through ten years with little rain. There had not been enough water for grass to grow very high. Short grass didn't offer much fuel for fires to burn. But the **drought** ended in 1996. Early that year it rained hard. So the grass grew thick and tall. When the rain ended, the tall grass dried out. By September, it was dry as well as high. The grass was the perfect fuel for fires.

Let It Burn

Even though most South Africans wanted the fires put out, park officials refused to do it. They said they would let the fires burn. The fires had been started by lightning strikes. So they were acts of nature. The officials said such fires should be allowed to burn. They believed it was nature's way of getting rid of the old and making way for the new.

The park is known for its different plants and animals, including giraffes.

New grass began to grow in the park after the fire.

"We would have only fought the fire if it had **threatened** one of the rest camps," said Chris van der Linde. Luckily, the fires never touched any of the buildings in the park or other places that people might camp or hike.

"This was a completely natural fire," added Bruce Bryden, another park official. "It was not a bad thing to have happened. It would be bad for the park if there were no fires. It's not as terrible as it seems."

After several more days, the fires finally died down on their own. By then, much of the park had been **blackened** by the fires. In these areas everything looked ugly and dead. All the plants had been burned. There didn't seem to be any animals left.

New Life

But then something wonderful happened. Within a few weeks, it began to rain. The water soaked the burned-out area. Suddenly, fresh grass began to pop

Not one animal died because of the fires.

out of the ground. Animals rushed to feed on this new grass. They seemed to like it better than the old grass in other parts of the park.

The fires had turned many trees black. But the trees did not die. A grass fire does not have enough heat to kill most trees. So even the blackened trees survived. They began to grow new leaves.

Not a single animal died because of the fires. "The animals knew what to do," said Chris van der Linde. "They made their way to rocky places or places around water holes." As the fires moved with the wind, so did the animals. They found patches of green grass here and there that were not burned. The fires had not **scorched** every inch of the park's ground. Somehow, the animals found the safe places.

Park officials were happy. They felt they had done the right thing. Harold Braack, the head of the park, said the fire "cleared the way for new growth. The park is very **healthy**."

No one could argue with him. Kruger National Park wasn't ruined. Today it remains one of the greatest wildlife parks in the world.

Read and Remember — Choose the Answer

Draw a circle around the correct answer.

1. What started the fires?

a car accident   lightning   a campfire

2. What did people fear the fires would do?

ruin the park   burn the city   kill firefighters

3. What helped the fires spread?

garbage dumps   thick grass   fast-moving storms

4. How many animals died in the fire?

none   about one hundred   too many to count

5. What happened to the burned-out area after it rained?

New grass grew.   Mudslides began.   Animals ran away.

Write About It

Imagine you are a park official at Kruger National Park. Write a letter to the editor of your local newspaper telling why you decided to let the fire burn.

Dear _____ ,

_____

_____

_____

_____

_____

_____

Focus on Vocabulary — Make a Word

Choose a word in dark print to complete each sentence. Write the letters of the word on the blanks. When you are finished, the letters in the circles will tell what people saw as the fire died out.

healthy   **percent**   **threatened**   **drought**   **blackened**

natural   **habitat**   **scorched**   **destroying**   **wildlife**

1. People wanted to save the animals' _____.

2. The park is the home of _____.

3. Officials said the fire was _____.

4. As much as 20 _____ of the park burned.

5. Many trees were _____ by the fire.

6. People worried the fire was _____ the park.

7. There had been a _____ in South Africa.

8. Today this national park is very _____.

9. The fire never _____ the rest camps.

10. The fire had not _____ every inch of ground.

Burnt Forests

A forest fire can burn land so much that it seems the forest will never grow back. But nature has a way of taking care of itself. In time, plants and animals live in the forest again. Study the diagram below. Write the answer to each question.

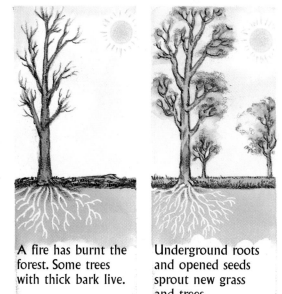

A fire has burnt the forest. Some trees with thick bark live.

Underground roots and opened seeds sprout new grass and trees.

As the grass and trees grow back, plant-eating animals return to the forest.

Meat-eating animals return to the forest to hunt food. The forest is healthy again.

1. What is the first event in the diagram? _____

_____

2. What keeps some trees from a fire? _____

3. Where do new grass and young trees come from? _____

_____

4. When would deer return to the forest? _____

_____

5. Why do meat-eating animals return to the forest? _____

_____

_____

The Death of an Island

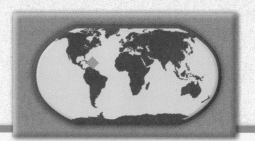

The island of Montserrat used to be called a **paradise**. It was surrounded by clear blue water. Its fields were a beautiful deep green. Everywhere fresh fruit grew and flowers bloomed.

About 11,000 people lived on this island in the Caribbean Sea. One of them was Winnie Saunders. Her family had been living on Montserrat for more than 100 years. In 1995 Saunders and her neighbors were told they should move. Then in 1997, their paradise became a **disaster zone.**

Some Leave, Some Stay

The island's problem was Soufrière Hills. That was the name of a volcano in the middle of the island. Soufrière Hills had not been **active** for 400 years. But on July 18, 1995, it sprang to life. It shot a bit of ash and steam high up into the air.

No one was hurt by the small eruption. Still, scientists **urged** people to get off Montserrat. They believed a much bigger blast could come any day.

The scientists were worried because the top of Soufrière Hills was made out of old lava. This top was called a **lava dome**. For a long time the dome had been **stable**. But now the insides of the volcano were bubbling again. Fresh lava could push up to the surface at any time. When it did, the old lava dome might break apart. That could send boiling ash and rocks flowing out across the island.

Some of Winnie Saunders's neighbors listened to the warnings. Over the next few months in 1995, about 7,000 people left their **beloved** island. Others

The people on Montserrat stared as the volcano erupted.

moved to the northern end of Montserrat. This end was **protected** from the volcano by large hills. There were not many houses or hotels there. Still, people squeezed in wherever they could. Many slept in tents or in church halls.

Still, others refused to go anywhere. They did not want to leave their homes. So they decided to take their chances with the volcano. Winnie Saunders was one of these people. Another was Virgie Sutton, an old family friend. "I'm staying right here," said Sutton.

Shaking a Soda

For two years, it looked like Saunders and Sutton had made a good choice. No big eruption came. Hot gas kept blowing out of Soufrière Hills. The volcano also sent out a few small rivers of ash. But that was it.

Still, scientists kept saying that the danger had not passed and that the people were living in a disaster zone. The lava dome was getting bigger. Fresh lava was building up in it. By the spring of 1997, the dome was more than half a mile high. Sooner or later, scientists believed, it would break open.

The gas coming out of the volcano was another bad sign. Scientist Mark Davies said to imagine shaking a soda bottle and then undoing the cap. "It **fizzes**. An eruption is like this," he said. The escaping gas was like the fizzing. It showed that the insides of the volcano were stirred up.

Deadly Waves of Ash

On June 25, 1997, Soufrière Hills did blow up. The top of the volcano exploded like a bomb. It was "like a huge mushroom cloud opening up," said Winnie Saunders. Ash and steam shot nine miles up into the sky.

Ash rained down from the sky, covering everything nearby.

Seconds later, waves of boiling hot ash, rocks, and steam came rushing down the side of the volcano. These waves were incredibly hot. They measured 1,800 degrees. The waves also moved very fast. Some traveled 90 miles per hour. In seven minutes, the burning waves buried several villages and killed 19 people. "They never had a chance," said Saunders.

Winnie Saunders was lucky. The hot ash and rocks swept by her house but didn't touch it. Virgie Sutton was not so lucky. She was killed by the burning flow.

Over the next few months, the volcano spit out more streams of ash and rock. Soon two-thirds of the island was covered with a thick coat of grey ash. Only the northern end was still green.

Even so, no really big blast ever came. The June 1997 eruption blew away only five percent of the lava dome. Later eruptions were smaller still. Some people believe the volcano will just continue to have small eruptions that will send out little rivers of ash. In either case, Winnie Saunders's **homeland** is no longer an island of paradise.

After the eruption, Montserrat no longer looked like a paradise.

Read and Remember — Finish the Sentence

Circle the best ending for each sentence.

1. Soufrière Hills was the name of a _____.

city   small island   volcano

2. Scientists told people to _____.

leave the island   stay calm   move to a nearby river

3. Many people moved to _____.

Soufrière Hills   the northern end of Montserrat   Sutton

4. The rocks and ash that came out of the volcano were _____.

green and sticky   very hot   dripping wet

5. Some people think the volcano will _____.

disappear   explode again   make Montserrat better

Think About It — Find the Main Ideas

Underline the two most important ideas from the story.

1. The eruption of a volcano ruined much of Montserrat.

2. Virgie Sutton was an old family friend of Winnie Saunders.

3. Most people have left the island of Montserrat.

4. Montserrat was surrounded by clear blue water.

5. Winnie Saunders's family had been living on Montserrat for more than a hundred years.

Focus on Vocabulary — Match Up

Match each word with its meaning. Darken the circle beside the correct answer.

1. paradise

○ not well known   ○ perfect place   ○ busy island

2. disaster zone

○ place with damage   ○ hard to find   ○ houses

3. active

○ doing something   ○ noticed   ○ getting higher

4. urged

○ said with force   ○ forgot to say something   ○ found

5. lava dome

○ top of a volcano   ○ hot mud   ○ field

6. stable

○ not changing   ○ easy to break   ○ hard to see

7. beloved

○ curved   ○ well loved   ○ loud

8. protected

○ complained about   ○ moved outward   ○ kept safe

9. fizzes

○ moves quickly   ○ loses   ○ makes a bubbling sound

10. homeland

○ house   ○ country where someone lives   ○ shore

Volcano Types

There are three main types of **volcanoes**. The volcanoes might be cone-shaped or dome-shaped. They might be made of layers, like the Montserrat volcano. Study the diagrams of three volcano types. Write the answer to each question.

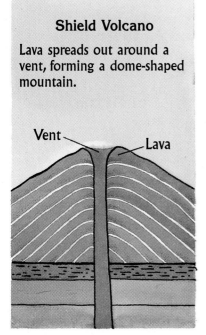

Shield Volcano

Lava spreads out around a vent, forming a dome-shaped mountain.

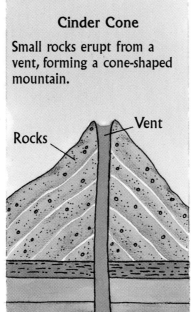

Cinder Cone

Small rocks erupt from a vent, forming a cone-shaped mountain.

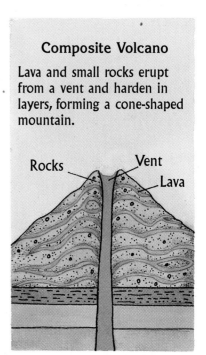

Composite Volcano

Lava and small rocks erupt from a vent and harden in layers, forming a cone-shaped mountain.

1. In which volcano does lava spread out from a vent? _____

2. Which volcano has layers of lava and rocks? _____

3. Does a shield volcano have a dome or cone shape? _____

4. Which volcano sends out mainly small rocks? _____

5. What shape does a composite volcano have? _____

6. What kind of volcano is the Montserrat volcano? _____

101

GLOSSARY

Words with this symbol can be found in the SCIENCE CONNECTION.

absorbed　page 56
Absorbed means taken in or soaked up.

acres　page 79
Acres are units for measuring land. An acre equals 43,560 square feet.

active　page 95
Active means moving. An active volcano is able to explode.

activity　page 31
Activity means movement or being active.

aluminum　page 82
Aluminum is a silver-white, light metal that is easy to make into different shapes.

announcers　page 47
Announcers are people who read the news, introduce programs, or give out information for radio and television stations.

ash　page 31
Ash is the fine powder that fills the air and falls to the ground when a volcano erupts.

assumed　page 47
Assumed means took for granted or supposed that a fact is true.

astronauts　page 74
Astronauts are people trained to travel in outer space.

astronomers　page 55
Astronomers are scientists who study the stars and planets of outer space.

atomic bomb　page 64
An atomic bomb is a very powerful, dangerous weapon.

attracted　page 56
Attracted means pulled toward.

beloved　page 95
Beloved means loved very much.

blackened　page 89
Blackened means made black.

blaze　page 8
A blaze is a strongly burning fire.

bolt　page 39
A bolt is a flash of lightning.

caddie　page 15
A caddie is a person who carries golf clubs for golfers.

canyons　page 71
Canyons are deep valleys with steep sides.

cells　page 42
Cells are the smallest parts of the body. Each part of the body is made up of a large number of cells.

challenge　page 82
A challenge is something that is difficult to do.

clogged　page 31
Clogged means filled or plugged up.

coal　pages 24, 29
Coal is a black rock found within the earth. It is usually used as fuel.

collapse　page 49
To collapse means to fall down.

102

conductors   page 45
Conductors are things that move electricity, heat, or sound.

conscious   page 17
Conscious means awake and aware of what is going on.

controls   page 8
Controls are instruments, such as handles or steering wheels, used to guide a machine.

convinced   page 64
Convinced means made people believe or agree to the truth of a fact or a statement.

core   page 37
The core is the innermost part of Earth.

courage   page 79
Courage means a will to carry on or keep going in spite of danger or hard times.

create   page 65
To create means to make.

crust   page 37
The crust is the top layer of Earth. The ground is the crust.

damage   page 16
Damage is harm caused by injury to one's body or property.

degrees   page 55
Degrees are units of measure for temperature or distance.

dense   page 33
Dense means thick or packed close together.

destroying   page 87
Destroying means ruining or putting an end to something.

disaster zone   page 95
A disaster zone is a place where terrible events happen suddenly and cause great damage.

dormant   page 63
Dormant means quiet or not active.

drought   page 88
A drought is a long time without any rain.

electricity   page 16
Electricity is a very strong form of energy.

ember   page 71
An ember is a small piece of glowing wood or coal from a fire.

engineer   page 7
An engineer is a person who operates or runs an engine, such as a train engine.

erupted   page 31
Erupted means exploded.

eruption   page 48
An eruption is a burst or an explosion of something, such as gases or rocks from a volcano.

evil   page 24
Evil is something that causes harm or trouble.

explosion   page 34
An explosion is the act of blowing up or breaking up with great force and noise.

Fahrenheit   page 23
Fahrenheit is a thermometer scale on which freezing is 32°F and boiling is 212°F.

firebreak   page 80
A firebreak is a strip of land that has been cleared to stop the spread of fire.

fireproof   page 82
Fireproof means something that does not burn or is not easily destroyed by fire.

fizzes   page 97
Fizzes means makes a hissing or bubbling sound.

front   page 55
A front is where cold air and warm air meet.

fuel   pages 7, 29
Fuel is a material that burns and is used to make heat or power.

funnels   page 72
Funnels are objects that direct something from a large area to a small area.

fuse   page 13
A fuse is a material that burns easily.

geologists   page 31
Geologists are scientists who learn about the layers of the earth, especially by studying rocks.

government   page 26
Government is a body of people who rule a community by making laws and providing services.

grounded   page 56
Grounded means to have a safe electrical connection to the ground.

gusts   page 71
Gusts are sudden, strong bursts of wind.

habitat   page 87
A habitat is a place where an animal or a plant usually lives.

healthy   page 90
Healthy means being in good health or being well.

homeland   page 98
A homeland is the area or the country where a person was born or grew up.

horror   page 39
Horror means great fear.

hydrants   page 74
Hydrants are pipes that are connected to main water lines. Firefighters get their water from hydrants.

ignited   page 7
Ignited means caught fire or started to burn.

incredibly   page 80
Incredibly means amazingly or very hard to believe.

lahar   page 47
Lahar is hot mud formed when a volcano erupts.

lava   page 33
Lava is melted rock that comes from a volcano.

lava dome   page 95
A lava dome is the top layer of an old lava bed.

lightning   pages 15, 21, 45, 85
Lightning is a flash of light made by a natural flow of electricity in the air.

lightning rod   page 56
A lightning rod is a metal pole that runs from the roof of a building into the ground.

liquid   page 47
A liquid is something that can flow.

lungs   page 40
Lungs are parts of the body used for breathing air.

magma   pages 47, 53
Magma is melted rocks and hot gases.

mantle   page 37
The mantle is the layer of Earth below the crust and above the core.

map key   page 61
A map key explains what the symbols or colors on a map mean.

medical   page 39
Medical means having to do with the practice of medicine.

moisture   page 71
Moisture means wetness.

movements   page 42
Movements are actions.

mudslides   page 65
Mudslides are soft, wet earth that move down the sides of hills or mountains.

natural   page 87
Natural means made by nature.

natural disasters   page 50
Natural disasters are terrible events that are caused by nature, such as hurricanes or floods.

numb   page 57
Numb means having no feeling. A person who is numb cannot feel heat, cold, or touch.

officials   page 23
Officials are people in charge.

oxygen   pages 25, 29
Oxygen is a gas that is found in air. Animals and people need to breathe oxygen in order to live.

panic   page 31
Panic is a sudden and very powerful feeling of fear.

paradise   page 95
Paradise is a place of great happiness and perfect beauty.

percent   page 87
A percent is one part in 100. One half of something is 50 percent.

plastered   page 10
Plastered means covered or coated.

plates   page 69
The plates are large pieces of Earth's rocky ground.

poisonous   page 23
Poisonous means causing sickness or death with poison.

porter   page 9
A porter is a person who carries suitcases or equipment.

predict   page 63
To predict means to guess or tell what is going to happen before it occurs.

professional   page 15
A professional is a person who is an expert paid to do a job, or play a sport.

swelling   page 40

Swelling means growth in size.

threatened   page 89

Threatened means gave signs of danger.

thunderstorm   page 15

A thunderstorm is a rainstorm that occurs with thunder and lightning.

tournament   page 15

A tournament is a contest played by at least two people in a sport or game.

tragedy   page 50

A tragedy is a very unhappy or terrible event.

tunnels   page 25

Tunnels are underground paths or roads.

unbelievable   page 58

Unbelievable means cannot be believed.

urged   page 95

Urged means tried to talk people into doing something.

vapor   page 9

Vapor is the gas form of something that is usually a liquid, such as water. In the air, it might look like a cloud or mist.

volcano   pages 31, 37, 53, 69, 101

A volcano is a hole in Earth's crust that can explode with lava, gases, hot rocks, or ash.

weather map   page 61

A weather map shows the kind of weather to expect in an area.

wildfires   page 79

Wildfires are dangerous fires that spread very quickly.

wildlife   page 87

Wildlife is wild animals that live in areas where there are no people.

Did You Know?

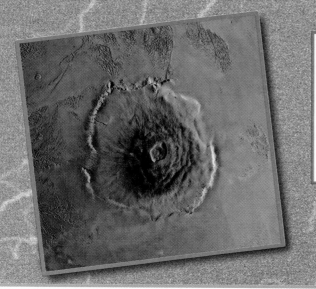

◀ Where is the largest known volcano? Olympus Mons is a volcano on the planet Mars. It measures more than 300 miles across at its base and is more than 14 miles high!

Have you ever noticed that you can see lightning before you hear the thunder it makes? This is because light travels much faster than sound. If it takes five seconds to hear thunder after you see lightning, the lightning was one mile away. ▶

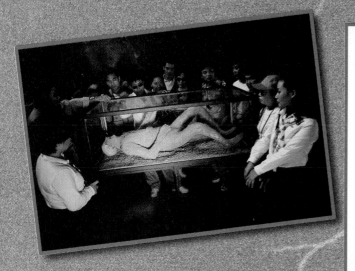

◀ Did you know a volcano can tell us about history? In A.D. 79 Mount Vesuvius in Italy erupted. It buried the Roman city of Pompeii 60 feet deep under ash and dust. More than 1,600 years later, scientists found buildings, streets, and places where people of Pompeii once lived. This buried city has helped us learn about the Roman way of life!

Where was the loudest volcano explosion in history? On August 27, 1883, a large volcano erupted on the island of Krakatoa in the Pacific Ocean. It blew up most of the island. The noise was so loud that it was heard 3,000 miles away!

Have you ever wondered what was the worst fire ever? In May 1987, a terrible fire burned across more than 18 million acres of pine forest in China and Russia. It lasted for more than a month. It caused billions of dollars worth of damage. The fire was so bad that people called it the Great Black Dragon Fire.

What are some amazing facts about lightning? The bright spark we see travels at the speed of light. That's more than 186,000 miles per second! Also, lightning can heat the air in its path to more than 60,000 degrees. That is hotter than the surface of the sun!

CHART YOUR SCORES

Score Your Work

1. Count the number of correct answers you have for each activity.
2. Write these numbers in the boxes in the chart.
3. Give yourself a score (maximum of 5 points) for **Write About It**.
4. Add up the numbers to get a final score for each tale.
5. Write your final score in the score box.
6. Compare your final score with the maximum score given for each story.

Tales	Read and Remember	Think About It	Write About It	Focus on Vocabulary	Science Connection	Score
Race Through the Flames						/24
Trouble on the Golf Course						/23
The Fire That Keeps Burning						/25
A Deadly Surprise						/23
Hit by Lightning						/26
Buried in the Night						/26
No Place to Hide						/23
Escape from a Volcano						/26
Wind and Fire						/25
Firefighters in Danger						/23
Nature's Fire						/25
The Death of an Island						/23

110